COLLECTION OF THE MOST BEAUTIFUL POEMS BY XU ZHIMO

《徐志摩诗歌精选集》系列
志摩最美的诗

Translators: LU Wenyan et al. Editors: Zilan et al.

译者：陆文艳 等 编辑：子岚 等

英国剑桥康河出版社
CAM RIVERS PUBLISHING

XU Zhimo, LIN Huiyin and Rabindranath Tagore in China, 1924

1924 年，徐志摩、林徽因、泰戈尔在中国合影留念

Contents

目录

Foreword

It is a pleasure and an honour to write a brief foreword to this collection of some of the most beautiful poems by Xu Zhimo, one of the greatest modern Chinese poets.

Xu's life and work were central to the first great opening up of China to Western artistic and literary influences during the quarter century after the establishment of the Republic of China in 1911. During that period, the country, which had been largely separated from the West, witnessed an incoming flood of philosophical, educational, aesthetic, scientific, literary and scholarly ideas from the West, not dissimilar in force to the great tidal waves that occur seasonally near Xu's home city of Haining.

The force of Xu's impact was the result of several intersecting pieces of good fortune, which set the context for his brilliant mind and personality. They crystallised in the two years he spent at King's College from 1921 to 1922.

Cambridge at that time was just recovering from the horrors of World War I. It was filled with great scientists, anthropologists, philosophers, and writers. In particular, there was the Bloomsbury Group with its joint attachments to London and King's College. Over the years its members included the economist John Maynard Keynes, the writers Virginia Woolf and E.M. Forster, and the artists Duncan Grant and Roger Fry. Several Bloomsbury Group intellectuals became Xu's close friends and mentors.

It was indeed a heady mixture: new ideas; the deep friendship of a number of older men schooled in the Old Etonian-King's College tradition of counting deep friendship as one of the great arts of life; the beauties of nature crafted by art, the sudden encounter with the Romantic poets, whose poetry had long been largely unknown in China.

Xu incorporated all this into his most famous poem, A Second Farewell to Cambridge written after his third visit to Cambridge in 1928. In this nostalgic poem, he created an image of Cambridge as the home to more beauty and interesting ideas than almost anywhere else on earth.

Xu's passion for Cambridge also recast the way the British saw their own country; he showed them that it did not consist solely of overpopulated commercial centres. He was the first Chinse to write with great feeling about British architecture and landscapes, and that, in turn, inspired the British to see their country with new eyes again.

As China and the West again merge, Xu Zhimo stands as a symbol of mutual curiosity and the desire to fuse the best of these two contrasting worlds. His charming poems serve a perfect bridge between China and the UK.

Professor Alan Macfalane

Emeritus Professor of Anthropology
Fellow of King's College, University of Cambridge
Fellow of the British Academy

前言

为中国最伟大的现代诗人之一徐志摩的最美诗歌选集撰写前言，我深感荣幸。

1911 年中国共和国成立之后的四分之一个世纪期间，中国初次对西方艺术和文化实行重大的开放，徐志摩的生活和工作是其中重要的一部分。经历了很大程度上和西方的隔离之后，在那期间，中国见证了来自西方如潮水般的哲学、教育、美学、科学、文学和学术方面的思想，在力度方面和徐志摩家乡季节性的海宁大潮无异。

徐志摩的影响力源于一些交叉的好运，它们奠定了他的精彩思想和个性的背景，在他于剑桥大学国王学院度过的两年时间中结晶（1921 - 1922）。

在那个时候，剑桥正处于第一次世界大战恐惧的恢复中。当时剑桥集中了诸多伟大的科学家、人类学家、哲学家和作家，其中包括和伦敦及国王学院有着共同联系的布鲁姆斯伯里团体。多年来，团体的成员包括经济学家约翰·梅纳德·凯恩斯、作家弗吉尼亚·沃尔夫以及画家邓肯·格兰特和荣格·弗莱。布鲁姆斯伯里的好几个成员都成为他的密友及导师。

这的确是一个让人陶醉的集合体：新思想；和一些伊顿 - 国王学院出身的年长者之间的深厚友谊 - 这两个学府都把深厚友谊看作是生活中了不起的艺术之一；艺术造就的自然魅力以及和一些在中国鲜为人知的浪漫主义诗人的突然相遇。

徐志摩把这一切都凝聚在他最著名的诗歌《再别康桥》中，该诗创作于他在 1928 年第三次拜访剑桥之后。在这首充满怀旧情怀的诗歌中，他把剑桥塑造成了一个世界上最有魅力以及思想最有趣的地方。

徐志摩对剑桥的激情也改变了英国人看待他们自己国家的方式；他给他们展示了一个不一样的英国，不再是一个集中了人口过多的商业中心的国家。他是第一个怀着深情描述英国建筑和景观的中国人，从而，给了英国人灵感，对自己的国家刮目相看。

当中国和西方再次交汇之时，徐志摩成为东西方共同的对彼此的好奇以及融合两个相异世界之间最好之处的渴望的一个标志。他的充满魅力的诗歌成为连接中国和英国之间的一个完美的桥梁。

艾伦·麦克法兰 教授

剑桥大学社会人类学教授
剑桥大学国王学院院士
英国国家学术院院士

Introduction

Xu Zhimo (January 15, 1897 – November 19, 1931) was one of the most renowned Romantic poets of 20th-century Chinese literature. He was a pioneering thinker who strove to loosen Chinese poetry from its traditional forms, and to reshape it under the influences of Western poetry and the vernacular Chinese language. His contribution to the promotion of Chinese poetry was phenomenal, as one of the first Chinese writers to successfully naturalize Western Romantic forms into modern Chinese poetry.

Xu Zhimo studied in England at King's College, Cambridge, where he fell in love with the English Romantic poetry of Keats and Shelley, and was also influenced by the French Romantic and Symbolic poets, some of whose works he translated into Chinese. In 1922 he returned to China and became a leader of the modern poetry movement.

Upon his return to China, Xu Zhimo started writing nostalgic poems about Cambridge as well as essays in the vernacular style. In 1923, he founded the Crescent Moon Society, inspired by the Indian poet Rabindranath Tagoire, for whom he served as an interpreter during a lecture tour in China. The foreign literature to which Xu Zhimo had been exposed served to shape his own poetry and establish him as a leader in the modern poetry movement in China, in particular the Crescent Moon style; his works helped bring about major changes to Chinese literature from that period.

During the last years of his life, he worked as an editor for several literary magazines and a professor at various higher education establishments, including Nanjing University and Peking University. Xu perished in a plane crash on November 19, 1931 near Tai'an, Shandong while flying en route between Nanjing and Beijing. He left behind four collections of verse and several volumes of literary translations from different languages.

Among all the foreign cities Xu visited, he always felt a special attachment to Cambridge, and often reflected on the impact of the many long walks and lively discussions and drinking sessions with fellow Cambridge intellectuals which together contributed to the development of his thinking and poetry. In July 2008, a white granite stone was installed by the river at King's College to commemorate Xu's time there, carved with the best-known lines from his most famous poem, A Second Farewell to Cambridge. The stone has become a Cambridge landmark, attracting Xu's admirers from all over the world.

Cam Rivers Publishing are extremely proud and pleased to publish this collection of some of Xu Zhimo's most beautiful poems in the original Chinese, together with English translations. We have endeavoured to present the most authentic and precise translation and maintain the unique charm of Xu's poetry.

All the poems in this collection have been meticulously selected from the four collections of Xu Zhimo's poetry: The Poems of Zhimo, One Night in Florence, Tiger and The Floating Clouds.

Editorial Team
Cambridge, July 2018

简介

徐志摩（1897年1月15日－1931年11月19日）是二十世纪中国文学界最著名的浪漫主义诗人之一。他是一个先锋的思想者，致力于把中国诗歌从传统形式中解放出来，并且在西方诗歌和中国白话文影响下，重塑形式。作为把西方浪漫主义形式移植到中国诗歌之中的先驱者之一，他对中国诗歌的宣传推广的贡献是非凡的。

在剑桥国王学院学习期间，徐志摩深深爱上了济慈和雪莱的英国浪漫主义诗歌，他也受到法国浪漫主义和象征主义诗人的影响，曾经把其中一些诗人的作品翻译成汉语。他在1922年回国，成为中国现代诗歌运动的领袖。

回国后，徐志摩开始以白话文写作有关剑桥的怀旧诗歌以及散文。他在印度诗人拉宾德拉纳d特·泰戈尔在中国巡回讲学期间担任翻译，受泰戈尔诗歌启发，于1923年创立新月社。

徐志摩接触的外国文学助他重塑他自己的诗歌，也创立了他在中国现代诗歌运动中的领袖地位，尤其是新月派；他的作品对促成中国文学在该时期的重大变化起到了带动作用。

在徐志摩的最后岁月里，他在几家文学杂志担任编辑，并且在一些大学担任教授，包括南京大学和北京大学。1931年11月19日，在从南京去北京的途中，徐志摩乘坐的飞机在山东泰安附近坠毁，一代诗人从此告别人间。

在徐志摩拜访过的所有外国城市中，他对剑桥始终有一种特别的归属感，经常回忆思索那些和剑桥知识分子朋友们一起进行的悠长散步、充满活力的讨论和小酌，这些都有助于他思想和诗歌的发展。

在2008年7月，一块白色大理石被安置于国王学院内的河边，纪念徐志摩在剑桥的日子，上面雕刻着《再见康桥》中最脍炙人口的诗句。这块大理石已经成为剑桥的一个地标，吸引着来自于世界各地的徐志摩的仰慕者。

剑桥康河出版社怀着骄傲和喜悦之情，推出徐志摩最美诗歌选集（中英文对照版）。我们尽力呈上最真实和精确的翻译，并且保持徐志摩原诗的独特魅力。

选集中所有的诗歌，精心选择于以下徐志摩诗歌集：《志摩之诗》、《翡冷翠的一夜》、《猛虎集》和《云游》。

编委会
2018 年 7 月于剑桥

Poems

诗集

By Chance

Translated by YANG Duhan

I am a cloud in the sky,
By chance casting my shadow in the waves of your heart –
No need to be surprised,
Or even show your delight –
In a twinkling I will disappear.
You and I meet on the sea of a dark night,
Facing in different directions.
You might remember,
But you'd better forget
How we shone in each other's eyes.

偶然

我是天空里的一片云，
偶尔投影在你的波心——
你不必讶异，
更无须欢喜——
在转瞬间消灭了踪影。

你我相逢在黑夜的海上，
你有你的、我有我的、方向；
你记得也好，
最好你忘掉，
在这交会时互放的光亮！

I Am in Love

Translated by LU Wenyan

I am in love;
I love the shining stars in the sky;
I love their crystalline presence:
There are no such Gods on the earth.

At dusk on a chilly evening in the depths of winter,
On a lonely grey early morning.
At sea, atop the mountain after the wind and rain –
There is always one star, ten thousand shining stars!

The intimacy of small grass flowers by the mountain stream,
The children's joy in the tall building,
The dazzling lights and compasses of the travellers;
The flashing fairies from one million miles away!

I have a shattered soul,
Like a pile of shattered crystal,
Scattered in the bleached grass of the wild –
Drinking in your fleeting attentiveness.

Of the now cold passion and tenderness in life,
I have also tasted the flavour and tolerated it;
At times the crickets' autumn song beneath the brick steps
Leads my heart to break, and forces me to weep.

I expose my honest mind,
Offer my love to the bright star of a single day,
Let life be fantasy or truth,
Let the earth exist or disappear –
There are vivid shining stars in space forever!

我有一个恋爱

我有一个恋爱；——
　我爱天上的明星；
　我爱他们的晶莹：
人间没有这异样的神明。

　在冷峭的暮冬的黄昏，
　在寂寞的灰色的清晨。
在海上，在风雨后的山顶——
　永远有一颗，万颗的明星！

　山涧边小草花的知心，
　高楼上小孩童的欢欣，
旅行人的灯亮与南针：——
　万万里外闪烁的精灵！

　我有一个破碎的魂灵，
　像一堆破碎的水晶，
散布在荒野的枯草里——
　饱啜你一瞬瞬的殷勤。

　人生的冰激与柔情，
我也曾尝味，我也曾容忍；
　有时阶砌下蟋蟀的秋吟，
　引起我心伤，逼迫我泪零。

我袒露我的坦白的胸襟，
　献爱与一天的明星，
　任凭人生是幻是真
　地球在或是消派——
大空中永远有不昧的明星！

Floating Clouds

Translated by LU Wenyan

On such a day you float through the air with poise,
Free and graceful, you do not mean to stay
On the other side of the sky or in the far corner of the earth,
Your joy is an unrestrained idyll,
You care not – on the humble ground
There lies a slender stream; as your shining beauty
Embellishes the void of his soul while you pass by and
Electrifies him, he embraces your fair image closely.

What he embraces tightly is lingering worries,
As beauty will not remain constant in the picturesque scene;
What he wants, since you have flown over thousands of mountains,
Is to cast his shadow on the broad lake and sea!
He is wasting away over you, and that slender stream
Is wishing, wishing in vain, for you to wing your way back!

云游

那天你翩翩的在空际云游，
自在，轻盈，你本不想停留
在天的那方或地的那角，
你的愉快是无拦阻的逍遥，
你更不经意在卑微的地面
有一流涧水，虽则你的明艳
在过路时点染了他的空灵，
使他惊醒，将你的倩影抱紧。

他抱紧的是绵密的忧愁，
因为美不能在风光中静止；
他要，你已飞渡万重的山头，
去更阔大的湖海投射影子！
他在为你消瘦，那一流涧水，
在无能的盼望，盼望你飞回！

Language of Groaning

Translated by LU Wenyan& Sophie Song

I would like to celebrate the miraculous universe,
I would like to forget the worries in the human world,
Like a care free waxbill,
Singing at dawn, hopping at dusk –
If only she could always keep me company like a gentle breeze!
I wish my poems would flow like clear water,
I wish my heart were as relaxed as the fish in the pond;
But now my heart is full of anxiety,
Oh God! If you do not return life and freedom to her,
I will never enjoy any idyll!

呻吟语

我亦愿意赞美这神奇的宇宙，
我亦愿意忘却了人间有忧愁，
象一只没挂累的梅花雀，
清朝上歌唱，黄昏时跳跃；——
假如她清风似的常在我的左右！

我亦想望我的诗句清水似的流，
我亦想望我的心池鱼似的悠悠；
但如今膏火是我的心，
再休问我闲暇的诗情？——
上帝！你一天不还她生命与自由！

The Joy of a Snowflake

Translated by SHENG Xiangyu

If I were a snowflake
Flying elegantly in the half sky
I would follow my path
Soaring soaring soaring
The ground would be my destination

I would not venture into that ice-cold valley
I would not approach those remote hills
And I would not go up these deserted streets
Soaring soaring soaring
You see I have my path!

Flying into the half sky wondrously
With knowledge of the peaceful places
I wait for her to visit the secret garden
Soaring soaring soaring
Oh, her scent is of cherry blossom

As I am so light
I softly touch upon her dress
Becoming close to her gently beating heart
Melting melting melting
Melting into her gently beating heart

雪花的快乐

假如我是一朵雪花，
翩翩的在半空里潇洒，
我一定认清我的方向——
飞扬，飞扬，飞扬，——
这地面上有我的方向。
不去那冷寞的幽谷，

不去那凄清的山麓，
也不上荒街去惆怅——
飞扬，飞扬，飞扬，——
你看，我有我的方向！

在半空里娟娟的飞舞，
认明了那清幽的住处，
等着她来花园里探望——
飞扬，飞扬，飞扬，——
啊，她身上有朱砂梅的清香！

那时我凭借我的身轻，
盈盈的、沾住了她的衣襟，
贴近她柔波似的心胸——
消溶，消溶，消溶——
溶入了她柔波似的心胸！

Go!

Translated by LU Wenyan

Go, human world, go!
I stand alone on the peak of the mountain high;
Go, human world, go!
I face the infinite sky vault of heaven;
Go, young man, go!
Buried with vanilla in the valley deep;
Go, young man, go!
Sorrow flows to the flock of crows in the twilight sky.
Go, dreaming land, go!
I have broken the jade cup of fantasy;
Go, dreaming land, go!
I welcome the eulogy from the mountain wind and ocean swell with a smile.
Go, all sorts, go!
Before me lie high peaks thrusting through the sky;
Go, everything, go!
Before me lies an infinity of infinity!

去吧

去吧，人间，去吧！
我独立在高山的峰上；
去吧，人间，去吧！
我面对着无极的穹苍。

去吧，青年，去吧！
与幽谷的香草同埋；
去吧，青年，去吧！
悲哀付与暮天的群鸦。

去吧，梦乡，去吧！
我把幻景的玉杯摔破；
去吧，梦乡，去吧！
我笑受山风与海涛之贺。

去吧，种种，去吧！
当前有插天的高峰；
去吧，一切，去吧！
当前有无穷的无穷！

I Don't Know in Which Direction the Wind Is Blowing

Translated by Linda Sheen

I don't know in which direction
the wind is blowing –
I am in a dream,
Wandering in the gentle waves of the dream.

I don't know in which direction
the wind is blowing –
I am in a dream,
Her tenderness, my infatuation.

I don't know in which direction
the wind is blowing –
I am in a dream,
Sweetness is the glory of the dream.

I don't know in which direction
the wind is blowing –
I am in a dream,
Her betrayal, my sadness.

I don't know in which direction
the wind is blowing –
I am in a dream,
Heartbroken in the sorrow of the dream.

I don't know in which direction
the wind is blowing –
I am in a dream,
Darkness is the glory of the dream.

我不知道风是在哪一个方向吹

我不知道风
是在哪一个方向吹——
我是在梦中，
在梦的轻波里依洄。

我不知道风
是在哪一个方向吹——
我是在梦中，
她的温存，我的迷醉。

我不知道风
是在哪一个方向吹——
我是在梦中，
甜美是梦里的光辉。

我不知道风
是在哪一个方向吹——
我是在梦中，
她的负心，我的伤悲。

我不知道风
是在哪一个方向吹——
我是在梦中，
在梦的悲哀里心碎！

我不知道风
是在哪一个方向吹——
我是在梦中，
黯淡是梦里的光辉。

Away from Home

Translated by LU Wenyan

Tonight, there is half a waning crescent moon;
I want to hold her hands,
Walk to the places where there are bright moons –
The same clear light, I say, complete or incomplete.
There is a magnolia tree bearing some wilted flowers;
She is a flower addict,
I love to see her take pity on the flowers –
The same fragrance, she says, blooming flowers and wilted flowers.
In the deep shade there is a decrepit nightingale;
She has suffered from the autumn cold,
Not as fine as before –
I am about to die, she says, but I do not regret my passion!
But this nightingale, this tree of flowers, this half moon –
I pondered alone.
Facing my shadow -
Where is she, ah, why is she sad, faded, incomplete?

客中

今晚天上有半轮的下弦月；
　我想携着她的手，
　　往明月多处走——
一样是清光，我说，圆满或残缺。

园里有一树开剩的玉兰花；
　她有的是爱花癖，
　　我爱看她的怜惜——
一样是芬芳，她说，满花与残花。

浓阴里有一只过时的夜莺，
　她受了秋凉，
　　不如从前浏亮——
快死了，她说，但我不悔我的痴情！

但这莺，这一树花，这半轮月——
　我独自沉吟，
　　对着我的身影——
她在那里，阿，为什么伤悲，凋谢，残缺？

I Am Waiting for You

Translated by LU Wenyan

I gaze out at the dusky yellow,
As if gazing into the future,
My trembling heart has blinded my hearing.
Why haven't you arrived? My hope
Is left to bloom each moment.
I expect your steps,
Your laughing words, your face,
Your soft silky hair,
Waiting for your everything;
My hope is at every second
Bleaching to death – where are you?

I want you so much and my heart aches,
I want your flame-like smiles,
Want your supple waist.
The flying sparks in your hair and in the corner of your eye;
I have fallen into the air of obsession,
Like an island,
In the wild green sea swell, I am floating and sinking unconsciously …
Oh, I eagerly desire
Your arrival, desire
That beautiful magic queen of the night
Will bloom till the end of time!
Why aren't you coming, how can you bear it!
You really know, I know that you know,
That you have not come is a fatal blow for me,
Kills the sunny springtime which has now opened up in my life,
Makes the darkness as solid as the iron in the mine,
Presses my mind and my breath;
Kills the poor delicate sprouts of hope,
Give me, like a prisoner
To jealousy and misery, the embarrassment of being

我等候你

我等候你。
我望着户外的昏黄
如同望着将来,
我的心震盲了我的听。
你怎还不来? 希望
在每一秒钟上允许开花。
我守候着你的步履,
你的笑语, 你的脸,
你的柔软的发丝,
守候着你的一切;
希望在每一秒钟上
枯死——你在哪里?
我要你, 要得我心里生痛,
我要你火焰似的笑,
要你灵活的腰身,
你的发上眼角的飞星;
我陷落在迷醉的氛围中,
像一座岛,
在蟒绿的海涛间, 不自主的在浮沉……
喔, 我迫切的想望
你的来临, 想望
那一朵神奇的优昙
开上时间的顶尖!
你为什么不来, 忍心的!
你明知道, 我知道你知道,
你这不来于我是致命的一击,
打死我生命中乍放的阳春,
教坚实如矿里的铁的黑暗,
压迫我的思想与呼吸;

And the tragedy and cruelty of despair.
This could be insanity. Or it is insanity.
I believe I am truly insane;
But I cannot steer the wheel when the course is set,
The calm after the storm from all sides does not permit me to hesitate –
I cannot turn back,
Fate is driving and whipping me!
I also know this is likely a road
Leading to destruction,
But for you, for you,
I am willing for anything;
This is not merely my enthusiasm,
My sole surviving sense says so.
Insanity! I want to grind the lightness of being
So as to touch a woman's heart!
Want to win, and can win, no more than
Her teardrop,
Her passing heartache,
Perhaps half a sound of an indifferent, mocking smile;
But I am also willing, even if
The news of my breaking my body is spread
Towards her heart, as if spread
Towards a stubborn rock, and she thinks me
A rat in an underground cave, a worm,
I am still willing!
Mad enough to be genuine, it is unconditional,
Even God is unable to return someone
Who has a mad heart as a general
He sometimes returns a soldier who has reached the front line.

打死可怜的希冀的嫩芽，
把我，囚犯似的、交付给
妒与愁苦，生的羞惭
与绝望的惨酷。
这也许是痴。竟许是痴。
我信我确然是痴；
但我不能转拨一支已然定向的舵，
万方的风息都不容许我犹豫——
我不能回头，运命驱策着我！
我也知道这多半是走向
毁灭的路，但
为了你，为了你，
我什么都甘愿；
这不仅我的热情，
我的仅有理性亦如此说。
痴！想磔碎一个生命的纤维
为要感动一个女人的心！
想博得的，能博得的，至多是
她的一滴泪，
她的一声漠然的冷笑；
但我也甘愿，即使
我粉身的消息传给
一块顽石，她把我看作
一只地穴里的鼠、一条虫，
我还是甘愿！

In vain, all is in vain,
That you have not come is a reality which cannot be denied,
Although the flames in my heart are fuelled,
Hungry for your everything,
Your hair, your smiles, your hands and feet;
No fantasy and prayer
Can shorten the distance between us
By even an inch!
The dusky yellow outside has already
Condensed into the pitch black of night,
The ice and snow hang in the twigs of the trees,
The birdsong has faded,
Silence is the consistent universe mourning.
The hands on the clock ever make
Mysterious gestures, seemingly guiding,
As if with sympathy, as if mocking.
Whenever it strikes, to me, I hear
The death knell of my heart being buried alive.

痴到了真，是无条件的，
上帝也无法调回一个
痴定了的心如同一个将军
有时调回已上死线的士兵。
枉然，一切都是枉然，
你的不来是不容否认的实在，
虽则我心里烧着泼旺的火，
饥渴着你的一切，
你的发，你的笑，你的手脚；
任何的痴想与祈祷
不能缩短一小寸
你我间的距离！
户外的昏黄已然
凝聚成夜的乌黑，
树枝上挂着冰雪，
鸟雀们典去了它们的啁啾，
沉默是这一致穿孝的宇宙。
钟上的针不断的比着
玄妙的手势，像是指点，
像是同情，像的嘲讽，
每一次到点的打动，我听来是
我自己的心的
活埋的丧钟。

This Is a Cowardly World

Translated by LU Wenyan

This is a cowardly world:
It does not tolerate falling in love, it does not tolerate falling in love!
Wear your rich hair down,
Expose your pair of feet;
Come with me, my love,
Abandon this world
Sacrifice our love!

I am holding your hands,
Love, you follow me;
Let the thistles and thorns pierce our soles,
Let the hail split open our heads,
You follow me,
I am holding your hands,
We have escaped the prison, restoring our freedom!

Follow me,
My love!
The human world has fallen behind our backs,
– Take a look, isn't this a vast misty white ocean?
Vast misty white ocean,
Vast misty white ocean,
Infinite freedom, you and I are in love!

Follow my fingers and watch
The blue of a small star over that sky -
That is an island, there is green grass on the island,
Fresh flowers, beautiful animals walking and birds flying;
Come aboard this fast, light vessel
To reach the ideal heaven –
Falling in love, joy, freedom –
Farewell to the human world, forever!

这是一个懦怯的世界

这是一个懦怯的世界：
容不得恋爱，容不得恋爱！
披散你的满头发，
赤露你的一双脚；
跟着我来，我的恋爱，

抛弃这个世界
殉我们的恋爱！
我拉着你的手，
爱，你跟着我走；
听凭荆棘把我们的脚心刺透，
听凭冰雹劈破我们的头，
你跟着我走，
我拉着你的手，
逃出了牢笼，恢复我们的自由！

跟着我来，
我的恋爱！
人间已经掉落在我们的后背，——
看呀，这不是白茫茫的大海？
白茫茫的大海，
白茫茫的大海，
无边的自由，我与你与恋爱！

顺著我的指头看，
那天边一小星的蓝——
那是一座岛，岛上有青草，
鲜花，美丽的走兽与飞鸟；
快上这轻快的小艇，
去到那理想的天庭——
恋爱，欢欣，自由——
辞别了人间，永远！

The Charm of the Sea

Translated by LU Wenyan

One
'Girl, single girl,
Why are you loath to leave
The seaside at dusk?
Girl, go back home, girl!'
'Ah, no; I do not want to go home,
I love this evening breeze blowing.'
On the sandy beach, in the evening mist,
There is a girl wearing her hair loose,
Lingering, lingering.

Two
'Girl, the girl wearing your hair loose,
Why are you wandering
On this cold and lonely sea?
Girl, go back home, girl!'
'Ah no; you listen to me singing,
Great sea, I sing – come and harmonise with me.'
In the starlight, in the cool wind,
Softly flows the young girl's crisp voice.
High singing, low humming.

Three
'Girl, daring girl!
The black screen has been drawn,
There will be dangerous wind and waves now,
Girl, go back home, girl'
'Ah no; you watch me dancing into the air,
Learn form a seagull diving into the waves.'
In the dim night time light, on the beach,
A slim shadow is spinning fast
Swirling, swirling.

海韵

一
"女郎，单身的女郎，
　你为什么留恋
　这黄昏的海边？ ——
女郎，回家吧，女郎！"
"啊不；回家我不回，
我爱这晚风吹："——
　在沙滩上，在暮霭里，
　有一个散发的女郎——
　　　徘徊，徘徊。

二
"女郎，散发的女郎，
　你为什么彷徨
　在这冷清的海上？
女郎，回家吧，女郎！"
"啊不；你听我唱歌，
大海，我唱，你来和："——
　在星光下，在凉风里，
　轻荡着少女的清音——
　　　高吟，低哦。

三
"女郎，胆大的女郎！
　那天边扯起了黑幕，
　这顷刻间有恶风波——
女郎，回家吧，女郎！"
"啊不；你看我凌空舞，
学一个海鸥没海波："——
　在夜色里，在沙滩上，
　急旋着一个苗条的身影——
　　　婆娑，婆娑。

Four
'Listen, the great sea's fury,
Girl, go back home, girl!
Look, the fierce mammal-like sea waves,
Girl, go back home, girl!'
Ah no; the waves won't swallow me,
I love the great sea's wildness!'
In the sound of the tides, in the light of the waves,
Ah, a panicked young girl is in the sea foam,
Hesitating, hesitating.

Five
'Girl, where are you, girl?
Where, your loud singing?
Where, your graceful shadow?
Where, ah, brave girl?'
The dark night has engulfed the brilliance of the stars,
There is no more radiance at this side of the sea,
The sea tides have engulfed the beach,
There is no more trace of the girl on the beach,
No more trace of the girl!

四

"听呀，那大海的震怒，
　女郎回家吧，女郎！
看呀，那猛兽似的海波，
　女郎，回家吧，女郎！"
"啊不；海波他不来吞我，
　我爱这大海的颠簸！"
　在潮声里，在波光里，
啊，一个慌张的少女在海沫里，
　　蹉跎，蹉跎。

五

"女郎，在哪里，女郎？
在哪里，你嘹亮的歌声？
在哪里，你窈窕的身影？
在哪里，啊，勇敢的女郎？"
　黑夜吞没了星辉，
　这海边再没有光芒；
　海潮吞没了沙滩，
沙滩上再不见女郎，——
　　再不见女郎！

Waiting for the Cuckoo in the Moonlight

Translated by LU Wenyan

Take a look at the motionless shadow of the bridge,
Count the ripples of the inlaid mother-of pearl,
I have leant on the stone balustrade and warmed the moss growing on it,
But the moss has frozen the depths of my heart;
Moon, do not imitate a bride's shyness,
To cover your smooth, beautiful head with a satin duvet.
Last night you remained here too,
Will she allow you to come tonight or not?
Listen to the temple tower bell of the faraway village,
Like the light swell in my dream regurgitating and swallowing,
I miss you like the rise and fall of the tide,
Like the lone, aimlessly drifting and lurching boat.
The water is crystalline, the night is deep, my thought is long,
Where is the affectionate friend I long for,
The wind is growling, the willow is floating, the elm leaves are small,
The singing voice makes one reminisce at length,
And grieve over the passing of spring.

月下等杜鹃不来

看一回凝静的桥影，
数一数螺钿的波纹，
我倚暖了石栏的青苔，
青苔凉透了我的心坎；

月儿，你休学新娘羞，
把锦被掩盖你光艳首，
你昨宵也在此勾留，
可听她允许今夜来否？

听远村寺塔的钟声，
象梦里的轻涛吐复收，
省心海念潮的涨歇，
依稀漂泊踉跄的孤舟！

水粼粼，夜冥冥，思悠悠，
何处是我恋的多情友，
风飕飕，柳飘飘，榆钱斗斗，
令人长忆伤春的歌喉。

I have Come to the Bank of the Yangtze to Buy a Handful of Lotus Seed Pods

Translated by LU Wenyan

I have come to the bank of the Yangtze to buy a handful of lotus seed pods;
I peel the layers of lotus skin,
Watch the gulls fly before me,
Trying to hold back melancholy tears in my eye –
I miss you, I miss you, ah, little dragon!
I have a taste of the lotus seed, remembering our intimacy:
The heavy blinds not drawn in front of the stairs,
Shielding our joy and love with one heart.
I hear your promise again,
'Forever yours, my body, my soul.'
I have a taste of the lotus heart, and my heart is even more bitter;
I am startled and worried at night,
By the nightmare I cannot rid myself of.
Who knows my bitterness and pain?
You have harmed me, love, how can I endure my days like this?
But I cannot blame you for betraying me,
I cannot bear to imagine that you have changed,
My heart is merely soft:
You are mine! I still
Hold you tightly –
Unless the sky turns upside down –
But who can imagine a day like that?

我来扬子江边买一把莲蓬

我来扬子江边买一把莲蓬；
手剥一层层莲衣，
看江鸥在眼前飞，
忍含着一眼悲泪——
我想着你，我想着你，啊小龙！

我尝一尝莲瓤，回味曾经的温存：——
那阶前不卷的重帘，
掩护着同心的欢恋；
我又听着你的盟言，
"永远是你的，我的身体，我的灵魂。"

我尝一尝莲心，我的心比莲心苦；
我长夜里怔忡，
挣不开的恶梦，
谁知我的苦痛？
你害了我，爱，这日子叫我如何过？

但我不能责你负，我不忍猜你变，
我心肠只是一片柔：
你是我的！我依旧
将你紧紧的抱搂——
除非是天翻——
但谁能想象那一天？

That Last Day

Translated by LU Wenyan

In that year when the spring wind will return no more,
On that day when dry branches will regrow green twigs no more,
At that time in the sky there will shine no light,
Only the misty black bewitching atmosphere pervating
In the space where the sun, the moon, the stars have died;
On that day when all the standards have been overthrown,
At that time when all values have been reassessed:
Exposed in the awesome spirit of the final judgement
All the hypocrisy and vanity and void:
The naked souls are crawling in front of the Lord;
My love, at that time you and I need not panic,
Need not even appeal, debate injustice or hide away,
These hearts of yours and mine, like pure white twin lotus flowers on one stalk,
On the green stalk of love, standing graceful, happy, fresh and beautiful,
In front of the Lord, love is the only glory.

最后的那一天

在春风不再回来的那一年，
在枯枝不再青条的那一天，
那时间天空再没有光照，
只黑蒙蒙的妖氛弥漫着
太阳，月亮，星光死去了的空间；

在一切标准推翻的那一天，
在一切价值重估的那时间：
　　暴露在最后审判的威灵中
一切的虚伪与虚荣与虚空：
赤裸裸的灵魂们匍匐在主的跟前；——

我爱，那时间你我再不必张皇，
更不须声诉，辨冤，再不必隐藏，——
你我的心，象一朵雪白的并蒂莲，
在爱的青梗上秀挺，欢欣，鲜妍，——
在主的跟前，爱是唯一的荣光。

Sayonara – To a Japanese Lady

Translated by YAN Jinglan

The very softness in that simple bow,
Delicate as a lotus flower in zephyr blow,
fare thee well, and wish me well,
Sweet sorrow in the leave-taking now ----
Sayonara!

沙扬娜拉 – 赠日本女郎

最是那一低头的温柔，
象一朵水莲花不胜凉风的娇羞，
道一声珍重，道一声珍重，
那一声珍重里有蜜甜的忧愁 ——
沙扬娜拉！

Second Farewell to Cambridge

Translated by LIANG Yao, LIANG Choo and Mick Le Moignan

Quietly, quietly, I am leaving
Just as quietly as I came.
Gently, I wave goodbye
To the clouds in the Western sky.

The golden willow on the bank of the Cam
Stands like a bride in the sunset.
Her reflection shimmers in the water,
And ripples in my heart.

The rushes in the soft river bed
Sway and glisten underwater.
I'd gladly be a river reed
Tossed by the currents of the Cam.

In the shadow of the elm is a pool
Not of clear spring water,
But a rainbow from heaven
Crushed and crumpled among the duckweed
Leaving only a rainbow-like dream.

Searching for a dream?
Take a long pole and punt
Gently back towards the greenest of green grass
In a boat brimful of starlight,
Singing out loud in the splendour of the starlight.

I cannot sing aloud now.
The flute and pan-pipes of parting have gone silent.
Even the clamorous summer insects are hushed for me.
Silence tonight in Cambridge.

Quietly, quietly I am leaving
Just as quietly as I came.
Careful not to brush away with my sleeve
The faintest wisp of a cloud.

再别康桥

轻轻的我走了，
正如我轻轻的来；
我轻轻的招手，
作别西天的云彩。

那河畔的金柳
是夕阳中的新娘
波光里的艳影，
在我的心头荡漾。

软泥上的青荇，
油油的在水底招摇；
在康河的柔波里，
我甘心做一条水草

那树荫下的一潭，
不是清泉，是天上虹
揉碎在浮藻间，
沉淀着彩虹似的梦。

寻梦？撑一支长篙，
向青草更青处漫溯，
满载一船星辉，
在星辉斑斓里放歌

但我不能放歌，
悄悄是别离的笙箫；
夏虫也为我沉默，
沉默是今晚的康桥！

悄悄的我走了，
正如我悄悄的来；
我挥一挥衣袖，
不带走一片云彩。

译者

LU Wenyan

Ms Wenyan Lu holds the title of Master of Studies in Creative Writing from the University of Cambridge. She has worked in media, English/Chinese teaching, and translation/interpreting for over twenty years. She has excellent command of both Chinese and English.

Wenyan takes great interest in literary translation. Her most notable achievement is the official Chinese translation of Robert Macfarlane's award-winning Mountains of the Mind.

Wenyan's translation of selected poetry allows readers to enjoy the beauty of poetry.

陆文艳

陆文艳女士为剑桥大学创意写作硕士，多年从事媒体、英语/汉语教学和翻译工作。文艳具有扎实的文字基本功以及极强文字驾驭能力。

文艳对于文学翻译尤其感兴趣，译作包括英国著名作家、剑桥大学学者罗伯特·麦克法伦的获奖畅销书《心事如山》。文艳以其文字的精准和生动受到称赞和好评。

文艳的诗歌翻译，能让读者充分体验诗歌之美。

YAN Jinglan

Yan Jinglan graduated from Peking University and Manchester University, specialising in English Literature. She is currently Professor, PhD supervisor and Director of Australia Research Centre at East University of Science and Technology; she is Executive Member and Deputy Secretary of Shanghai Foreign Languages Committee; Executive Member of China Cross-Cultural Communication Research Committee, Deputy Director of Shanghai Committee, China Cross-Cultural Communication Research Centre; Executive Member of China Australia Research Committee; Executive Member of Shanghai Foreign Literature Committee; Executive Member of China English Newspaper & Magazine Research Committee.

Research interests: Cross-Cultural Communication, English, American & Australian Literature and English teaching. She has had more than 50 essays and over 20 books published, including text books and teaching reference books. She has translated The Famous Painter Monet and The Famous Painter Cezanne.

颜静兰

毕业于北京大学西语系英国语言文学专业和英国曼彻斯特大学语言文学专业，现为华东理工大学教授，博士生导师，硕士生导师，澳大利亚研究中心主任；上海市外文学会常务理事、副秘书长；中国跨文化交际研究会常务理事，中国跨文化交际研究会上海分会副会长；中国澳大利亚研究学会常务理事；上海外国文学学会常务理事；全国英语报刊研究会常务理事。

研究方向：跨文化交际、英美澳文学、英语教学。发表论文50多篇，出版的专著、教材、教辅等20多本，翻译作品有：《著名画家莫奈》；《著名画家塞尚》。

SHENG Xiangyu

Dr Xiangyu Sheng has over twenty years' experience, Dr Sheng is a Technical Director for the environment at a major multidisciplinary engineering consulting firm in the UK. She has a wide range of expertise in environmental science and climate change. She published a book titled "Air Dispersion Modelling in Regulatory Applications" and has over thirty publications. She is a Chartered Engineer (CEng) and a chartered Environmentalist (CEnv). She was a Co-Founder and Chair of the UK Chinese Association of Environment and Resources. She also served as Vice President of Federation of Chinese Professional Societies in the UK. She is an alumna of Newnham College, University of Cambridge. In her personal capacity, she is Chief Editor of "River Cam Breeze" Chinese Literature Journal.

盛湘渝

环境科学博士，在英国工作二十余年，现任英国某大型工程公司的环境总监，长期从事环境科学与气候变化的研究工作。著有"法规性大气扩散模型"一书并发表了30余篇学术论文。她曾为全英中国资源与环境协会联合创始人并曾任理事长，曾任中国留英学者专业团体联合会副主席。她是英国注册工程师（CEng）和注册环境师 (CEnv)。她是剑桥大学 Newnham College 校友。业余时间她任剑桥《剑河风》杂志社主编。

Linda Sheen

Linda Sheen, Chinese Name: JIANG Xin, Poet & Scholar, Academic Visitor at Faculty of English, University of Cambridge from Sep 2016 to Sep 2017; Member of Pembroke Poetry Society (Pem Soc); Member of Pelican Poets and Writers (PPWers); Member of River Cam Poetry Society; Editor of River Cam Breeze Magazine. Her first Poetry Collection 'Seeing Cambridge Again' (Chinese Version) has been published by Cam Rivers Publishing.

齐婉然

齐婉然，本名：蒋欣，英文名：Linda Sheen，学者，英国剑桥康河出版社签约诗人，著有诗集《又见康桥》。2016年9月至2017年9月期间为英国剑桥大学英文系访问学者；剑桥大学彭布罗克学院诗社成员；剑桥大学基督圣体学院鹈鹕诗人与作家协会会员；剑河诗社成员；《剑河风》杂志社编辑。

YANG Duhan

YANG Duhan is a current MPhil student majoring in Asian and Middle Eastern Studies at the University of Cambridge. She obtained her Bachelor's degree in English Language and Literature from Zhejiang University, China. She has published several essays about cultures and worldwide tourism development as a guest writer for the Chinese media Global Times. She participated as a translator in the translation work of King's College, Cambridge, Professor Alan Macfarlane's book How to Discover the World: Reflections for Rosa and his guide book on King's College: King's College Cambridge, a personal view.

杨杜菡

杨杜菡，剑桥大学亚洲与中东研究专业在读研究型硕士，本科毕业于浙江大学英语语言文学专业。作为中国媒体《环球时报》的特约作者，发表多篇有关世界文化与旅游发展类文章。曾作为第二译者参与翻译剑桥大学艾伦·麦克法兰教授著作《如何发现世界：给罗莎的信》。

Sophie Song

Sophie Song, poem lover.

宋熙

宋熙，诗歌爱好者。

Acknowledgements

致谢

We would like to show our appreciation by thanking the following organizations and individuals who have made this publication possible:

Vanishing Worlds Foundation
The team of the Cambridge Rivers Project, University of Cambridge
The City of Haining
Cambridge Chinese Community Centre
The grandson of Xu Zhimo, Tony Hsu, and his family
Professor LIU Zheng Cheng and his family
Professor WANG Keling & ZHONG Yuan
XIAO Rong and her family
WANG Hong & YANG Youming
HE Yanjin & XIANG Ke and their family
YANG Ke
XUE Yisha
WANG Kimmey Zihao and his family
Dr. SUN Wei
XU Zhengbiao

本书的顺利出版，仰仗于以下诸方的大力支持，在此我们献上诚挚的谢意：

英国保护濒临消失的世界基金会
剑桥大学康河计划工作人员
中国海宁市
剑桥华人社区中心
徐志摩嫡孙徐善曾博士及其家人
刘正成教授及其家人
王克陵教授及钟媛女士
肖融女士及其家人
王红女士 & 杨友明先生
何彦槿女士 & 向科先生及其家人
杨克先生
薛忆沙女士
王子昊先生及家人
孙伟博士
徐正标先生

CAM RIVERS PUBLISHING LTD

First published in Great Britain
By Cam Rivers Publishing Ltd 2018

Collection of the most Beautiful Poems by Xu Zhimo

Publisher: WANG Zilan
Honorary Chairman of Cam Rivers Xu Zhimo Project: Dr. Tony Hsu
Honorary Editor: Professor Alan Macfarlane FBA
Editor-in-Chief: WANG Zilan , Lucy Hamilton
Vice-Editor: LU Wenyan, WANG Keling
Assistant Editor: HE Wen

Senior Advisor: Tony Hsu (The grandson of XU Zhimo), LIU Zhengcheng,
                YANG Ke, GUAN Yunke
Advisor: LIU Chunchao, XIAO Rong, WANG Hong, SUN Wei,
         LIU Cynthia Yue, XU Zhengbiao
Sponsor: HE Yanjin, XUE Yisha, WANG Kimmey Zihao

Marketing Manager: James O'Sullivan, XUN Xiaoya
Assistant Marketing Manager: William Barlow, ZHANG Jinyu, Lya Simond
Contact: press@cambridgerivers.com

Book Design: Ning Li, AI Jiaqi
Translators: LU Wenyan, YAN Jinglan, LIANG Choo, SHENG Xiangyu   ,
YANG Duhan, Linda Sheen, Sophie Song

Design and Typeset: Moxi Studio
Chinese Marketing Consultant: Shanghai Cam Rivers Communications
Chinese Media Consultant: MUYE

Written content @ Author

Cam Rivers - Xu Zhimo Project is kindly supported by Xu Zhimo Family.

The publishing of this book is supported by Vanishing Worlds Foundation, U.K.

ISBN: 978-1-912603-14-5
www.cambridgerivers.com

英国剑桥康河出版社

2018 年首次在英国出版

《徐志摩诗歌精选集》系列之《志摩最美的诗》

作者：徐志摩
译者：陆文艳、颜静兰、梁莲珠、盛湘渝、杨杜菡、齐婉然、宋熙

本书属于"康河－徐志摩文创计划"。
本计划获得徐志摩家族特别支持，荣誉主席：徐善曾博士（徐志摩嫡孙）

荣誉主编：英国国家学术院院士、剑桥大学国王学院终身院士、
　　　　　剑桥大学社会人类学教授 艾伦·麦克法兰

主编：王子岚、露西·汉密尔顿

副主编：陆文艳、王克陵
编辑助理：何文

资深顾问：徐善曾、刘正成、杨克、关蕴科
顾问：刘春潮、肖融、王红、孙伟、刘月、徐正标
赞助人：何彦槿、薛忆沙、王子昊

市场推广主管：詹姆斯·沙利文、荀晓雅

市场推广助理：威廉·薛贝·巴尔珞、张瑨钰、Lya Simond
书籍设计：宁力、艾佳琦
装帧设计：摩西工作室
中国区推广：中国上海康河文化传播
中国区媒体推广：睦野

ISBN: 978-1-912603-14-5
网址：www.cambridgerivers.com
联系方式：press@cambridgerivers.com